Navigating through the Storms

of a Christian Life

Richard DeGiacomo

Editing and typesetting by Liz Smith of InkSmith Editorial Services

Cover photo © Can Stock Photo / Jurassic

Images courtesy of Sweet Publishing / New Harvest Ministries International (FreeBibleimages.org) and Free-Photos from Pixabay.

Navigating through the Storms of a Christian Life/Richard DeGiacomo

ISBN: 9781079281828

Contents

CONTENTS

Introduction

This book is intended for all people, those who believe in the majesty of God as well as those who have lost touch with Him, either completely or in some diminishing degree. It is also for those who want to strengthen their bond with the Almighty—and doing so will, through the divine power of the Holy Spirit, bring our Savior Jesus Christ into their daily life.

Life without Jesus is like being on a boat without a rudder in a violent and powerful storm. There is no way to stay on course. The boat goes this way and that way depending on the wind, waves, and currents. No steady direction can be maintained, and disaster is always present. When we bring Jesus into our life, our course of righteousness becomes clear. He is our rudder, and through His grace the storms of life can be confronted and defeated.

Is it time to give yourself totally to Jesus? That is a question only you can answer. *Yes* means total acceptance of who He is and His teachings and to thank Him for giving His life for our sins so that we who believe and repent will be saved. *No* will be a life without true meaning, a life of self-indulgence, a life without structure, filled with false happiness. *No* means eat, drink, and be merry without concern of this life or, more importantly, eternity.

Maybe it is time to give some thought to what happens when life as we know it is over. Is that it, or is there something else? Most people believe there is life after death and that life is eternal. We who believe in Jesus are 100 percent certain that when we pass on there will be either eternal salvation or eternal destruction.

Those are the choices. Salvation is heaven. Destruction is hell. The decisions we make during our lifetime will determine where eternity will be spent. Pick up the Holy Bible. Read His words and then make your choice. It's all there—the past, present, and future.

> For the things which are seen are temporary, but the things which are not seen are eternal.
>
> **– 2 Corinthians 4:18**

Now it is time to get on with life. Nothing can be done about past mistakes. No matter how much regret we have, the past can't be changed. If we are truly sorry and ask for forgiveness, we are forgiven. If God forgives us, why can't we forgive ourselves?

Learn from the past and move forward. Trust in Jesus, for He will never let you down. What we have control of is the present, and that is where Christian values take charge.

Life is full of complications and difficulties. Without spiritual guidance, our time on earth will be one of continuous turmoil. It will be a life of frustration, confusion, and self-indulgence, and we will seldom have inner peace. Although we seek and may find happiness, it will be temporary in nature, for the state of perfect eternal happiness can only be found in heaven.

With spiritual guidance from the Holy Spirit, we will be able to cope with the sorrows and disappointments that are natural to our human nature. Our foundation will be stronger as our faith and trust in the Lord continues to develop and guide us in making the right choices. We never will be given more than we can take, and Jesus will always be there for us.

> Come to Me, all you who labor and are
> heavy laden, and I will give you rest. Take
> My yoke upon you and learn from Me, for I
> am gentle and lowly in heart, and you will
> find rest for your souls. For My yoke is
> easy and My burden is light.
>
> – Matthew 11:28–30

Although things may look bleak, and at times it appears there is no way out, don't give up. If we give up, we are missing out on what God has planned for us. We are always in the hands of the Almighty and, therefore, are never alone. He will give us the strength to get through our difficulties if we ask for His help.

To give yourself totally to Jesus, you must believe He takes priority in all phases of your life. Total belief and trust in Him will result in a less stressful, more peaceful existence on earth. Our life on earth is measured in terms of years, but eternity can't be measured. It has no end. It is forever. We have two choices: eternal salvation or eternal destruction.

Jesus Fulfilled the Prophecies

Christianity is the pathway to eternal salvation. It begins with the many prophecies found in the Bible, prophecies that were fulfilled by the birth of Jesus, His ministry, crucifixion, resurrection, and ascension into heaven. This incredible story is God's plan for the salvation of mankind.

The thousands of prophecies in the Bible were God's way of communicating to humans through men called prophets. Their words were God's words. They told us what would happen over time, and it did.

Mark Cahill, in his book *One Heartbeat Away*, lists a few of the many prophecies found in the Bible relating to Jesus, the Messiah.[1] Each prophecy can be found in the Old Testament, and its fulfillment is stated in the New Testament:

God said He would bring forth a Son from a virgin, and He did:

Prophecy: Isaiah 7:14

Fulfillment: Matthew 1:18–25

God said that the Messiah would be the everlasting Father in human form, and He was:

Prophecy: Isaiah 9:6

Fulfillment: Acts 1:8–11; John 8:58

God said that He would have a Son, and He did:

Prophecy: Psalm 2:7

Fulfillment: Matthew 3:17; Matthew 17:5: Luke 22:66–71

God said His Son would be born in Bethlehem, and He was:

Prophecy: Micah 5:2

Fulfillment: Matthew 2:1

God said His Son pre-existed all things, and He did:

Prophecy: Micah 5:2

Fulfillment: John 8:56–58; Colossians 1:17

God said His Son would perform miracles, and He did:

Prophecy: Isaiah 35:6

Fulfillment: Matthew 9:35; Matthew 15:29–31

God said that Jesus would rise from the dead, and He did:

Prophecy: Psalm 16:10

Fulfillment: Acts 2:31

God said that His Son would be betrayed by a friend who ate with Him, and He was:

Prophecy: **Psalm 41:9**

Fulfillment: **Matthew 10:4; John 13:21–22, 25–26**

God said that the price of the betrayer would be thirty pieces of silver, and it was:

Prophecy: **Zechariah 11:12**

Fulfillment: **Matthew 26:15**

God said His Son would be crucified, and He was:

Prophecy: **Psalm 22:14–20**

Fulfillment: **Luke 23:33–34**

God said His Son would be pierced, and He was:

Prophecy: **Zechariah 12:10**

Fulfillment: **John 19:33–37**

God said that He would make the earth dark at noon, and He did:

Prophecy: **Amos 8:9**

Fulfillment: **Matthew 27:45**

(The Jewish clock began at 6 a.m., so the sixth hour was noon)

These are just a few of the thousands of prophecies found in the Bible. What is truly amazing is that they were made as far back as one thousand years before the birth of Christ.

The Ten Commandments

As Christians, we believe that God made His covenant with us through the Ten Commandments (**Exodus 20:1–17**). God gave the commandments to Moses to be the rules of law for the Israelites and all people.

After Moses's death, God appointed Joshua as Moses's successor. He told Joshua to lead the Israelites across the Jordan to the promised land. As soon as the priests carrying the ark of the covenant got to the river's edge, the waters parted, and the Israelites walked across on dry land. This was a repeat of what God did to the Red Sea forty years earlier.

God also suggested to Joshua that his people never forget the Ten Commandments, that they should be said daily so they wouldn't be forgotten. We should do the same.

It is interesting to note that when God presented the Ten Commandments to Moses, they were inscribed on two tablets of stone. The left side had the first three, which show the love of God, and the remaining seven, on the right side, show the love of mankind.

The Ten Commandments

1. I am the Lord your God; you shall not have false gods before me.

2. You shall not take the name of the Lord your God in vain.

3. You shall keep holy the sabbath day.

4. You shall honor your mother and father.

5. You shall not kill.

6. You shall not commit adultery.

7. You shall not steal.

8. You shall not bear false witness against your neighbor.

9. You shall not covet your neighbor's wife.

10. You shall not covet your neighbor's goods.

Many Christians are under the misconception that the importance of the Ten Commandments has been diminished since the coming of Jesus. That is totally false. Here is what the Bible has to say about the commandments of God:

> Do not think that I came to destroy the Law or the Prophets. I did not come to destroy but to fulfill.
> **– Matthew 5:17**

> For in my inner being I delight in God's law.
> **– Romans 7:22 NIV**

> Keeping the commandments of God is what matters.
> **– 1 Corinthians 7:19**

> If you want to enter into life, keep the commandments.
> **– Matthew 19:17**

Who Is Jesus?

Who is Jesus? He is God's only begotten Son. He is the Messiah (the chosen one). He is the earthly human extension of God the Father and, therefore, is God. Jesus had both divine and human natures.

Why did Jesus come to this earth as one of us?

- To further reveal God to humanity by words and deeds

- To fulfill the law of Moses

- To destroy the works of the devil

- To prepare us for a heavenly destiny

- To die for the sins of the world

What did He do?

- He talked continually with God the Father. "They came to a place which was named Gethsemane; and He said to His disciples, 'Sit here while I pray.'" (**Mark 14:32**)

- He acknowledged the importance of the Holy Spirit. (**John 14:16**)

- He obeyed the will of His heavenly Father. "For I have come down from heaven, not to do My own will, but the will of Him who has sent me." (**John 6:38**)

- He resisted temptation. (**Luke 4:1–13**)

- He reached out to the hopeless and sinners. (**Mark 2:15–17**)

Another question which has been asked numerous times is *What were the human characteristics of Jesus?* The conclusion of many historians is that since Jesus was a Jew, He therefore had Jewish features. His hair was short—long hair for a man was not acceptable. He had a beard. He was in very good physical condition, which can be attributed to his hard work as a carpenter and the continuous walking during His ministry. His facial expressions were warm and compassionate. He was of average height for that time, five feet five inches tall, and most likely had brown eyes, black hair, and olive-brown skin.

Jesus's divinity was clearly documented numerous times throughout the New Testament. One of many examples can be found in John 4 in the story of the Samaritan woman at Jacob's well. She told Jesus that she believed the Messiah was coming. Jesus said to her, "I who speak to you am He." (**John 4:26**) Other examples can be found in **John 10:30**, "I and My Father are one," and in **John 8:58,** "I say to you, before Abraham was, I AM."

Jesus always was and always will be. He was the greatest person ever to exist on this earth. He truly is God. The mystery of the Trinity—the Father, Son, and Holy Spirit, three in one—will never be understood by our finite human minds. It is based on revelation as documented in the Holy Bible and accepted as the truth because of our faith.

Wisdom, a Gift from God

Being a Christian is also using the gift of wisdom wisely. Wisdom is the ability to think and act using knowledge, experience, understanding, and common sense.

Wisdom is a gift from God. It comes from the Holy Spirit who dwells within us. It is through wisdom our heavenly reward will be realized. Without wisdom, we will live in spiritual darkness, which will not only affect our spiritual destiny but also the quality of our earthly existence.

Wisdom is knowledge and good judgment, and it gives us the ability to make the right choices throughout our entire life. Ask the Holy Spirit for guidance in making life choices.

> If any of you lacks wisdom, you should ask God, who gives generously to all without finding fault, and it will be given to you.
>
> — James 1:5 NIV

> Then I saw that wisdom excels folly, as light excels darkness.
>
> — Ecclesiastes 2:13

I would not possess wisdom unless God gave her to me.

— **Book of Wisdom 8:21 NRSV**

If you desire wisdom, keep the commandments, and the Lord will lavish her upon you.

— **Sirach 1:26 NRSV**

It is wisdom or the lack of wisdom that will affect the choices we make.

A wise man's heart is at his right hand, but a fool's heart at his left.

— **Ecclesiastes 10:2**

Do not forsake wisdom, and she will protect you; love her, and she will watch over you.

— **Proverbs 4:6 NIV**

The words of the reckless pierce like swords, but the tongue of the wise brings healing.

— **Proverbs 12:18 NIV**

Let the one who is wise heed these things and ponder the loving deeds of the Lord.

— **Psalm 107:43 NIV**

A person's wisdom yields patience; it is to one's glory to overlook an offense.

— **Proverbs 19:11 NIV**

Listen to advice and accept discipline, and at the end you will be counted among the wise.

— **Proverbs 19:20 NIV**

A fool vents all his feelings, but a wise man holds them back.

— **Proverbs 29:11**

How much better to get wisdom than gold! And to get understanding is to be chosen rather than silver.

— **Proverbs 16:16**

Submit to Jesus

The most important choice a person can make is to give oneself totally to Jesus, to confess all sins to Him with sincerity. We must acknowledge that we are sinners and thank Him for giving His life on the cross so we who truly believe in Him and have repented will be saved. **Mark 1:15** tells us that to enter into the kingdom of heaven, you must "repent, and believe in the gospel."

If you do believe in Jesus, ask for forgiveness. Let Him know you are truly sorry for offending Him.

Ask for His grace and strength to get you through the many trials of life. If you are truthful and sincere, your sins will be forgiven. Then it will be time to move forward and get on with life. Nothing can be done about the past. It cannot be changed, so don't dwell on it, but learn from it. If God forgives us, why can't we forgive ourselves?

We have no idea what the future will bring. What is going to take place will take place. Trust in Jesus and have faith. Put your future in His hands—He will not let you down. What we do have control of is the present, and that is where our commitment to Christian values takes charge. Life can be difficult at times, but as promised by Jesus, we will never be given more than we can handle, and He will always show us a way out.

> No temptation has overtaken you except such as is common to man; but God is faithful, who will not allow you to be tempted beyond what you are able, but with the temptation will also make the way of escape, that you may be able to bear it.
>
> — 1 Corinthians 10:13

> For the things which are seen are temporary, but the things which are not seen are eternal.
>
> — 2 Corinthians 4:18

19

Be strong and of good courage; do not be afraid, nor be dismayed, for the Lord your God is with you wherever you go.

– Joshua 1:9

To give yourself totally to Jesus, you must believe that He takes priority in every phase of your life. Total belief and trust in Him will result in a less stressful and more peaceful existence here on earth.

God the Father gave us the Ten Commandments to live by. At the Last Supper, Jesus told His apostles, "A new commandment I give to you, that you love one another; as I have loved you, that you also love one another" (**John 13:34**).

He went on to say that He must die on the cross. After three days, He would rise from the dead, and forty days later He would ascend into heaven. He did this for the salvation of mankind. It is because of His crucifixion, death, resurrection, and ascension into heaven that we can have eternal salvation. That is what Jesus promised each one of us.

As Christians, we accept the fact, based on Jesus's spoken word, that everyone will exist eternally either in heaven or hell. It is our life choices and God's mercy which will be the final determination. **John 3:14–15** says, "And as Moses lifted up the serpent in the wilderness, even so must the Son of Man be lifted up, that whoever believes in Him should not perish but have eternal life."

By Jesus assuming a human nature, He fulfilled the prophecies of His birth, ministry, death, and resurrection. **Isaiah 7:14** tells us "Therefore the Lord Himself will give you a sign: Behold, the virgin shall conceive and bear a Son, and shall call His name Immanuel." The meaning of *Emmanuel* is "God with us."

> Rejoice greatly, O daughter of Zion!
> Shout, O daughter of Jerusalem!
> Behold, your King is coming to you;

He is just and having salvation,
Lowly and riding on a donkey,
A colt, the foal of a donkey.

– Zechariah 9:9

He was despised and rejected by mankind, a man of suffering, and familiar with pain.

Like one from whom people hide their faces he was despised, and we held him in low esteem.

Surely he took up our pain and bore our suffering, yet we considered him punished by God, stricken by him, and afflicted.

– Isaiah 53: 3-4 NIV

The above readings from the Old Testament were spoken around five hundred to one thousand years before Christ's birth. All the revelations were given to the prophets chosen by God to be revealed to mankind. It was God's words they were speaking.

Jesus—Our Savior, Our Example

Jesus's earthly ministry was to preach the good news and to show us by example how to live our lives. God the Father didn't send Jesus into the world to judge the world, but that the world should be saved through Him. The message of salvation is very clear and is found throughout the New Testament. That message is love and forgiveness. He gave His life so that we would be saved, and He did it out of love for all.

Again at the Last Supper, Jesus told His apostles, "This is My commandment, that you love one another as I have loved you. Greater love has no one than this, than to lay down one's life for his friends. You are My friends if you do whatever I command you" (**John 15:12–14**).

Our salvation is based on obeying the Ten Commandments and the teaching of Jesus Christ. "For the law was given through Moses, but grace and truth came through Jesus Christ" (**John 3:17**). Not only do we need Jesus for our salvation, but it is *through* Him and believing *in* Him that we will have a life here on earth guided by His presence, filling us with the grace we need for a more peaceful and

23

rewarding existence. The amount of grace we can receive is unlimited. It is determined by prayer and actions. In other words, infrequent prayer produces a rain shower of grace whereas frequent prayer will result in a downpour of grace.

Life will always have its up and downs, as pointed out in **Ecclesiastes 3:1–8.** Getting through the difficult times can be a problem. However, with Jesus in our lives, those difficult times will be easier to cope with. He will always be there for us. All we should do is ask for His help. **Matthew 11:28** says, "Come to Me, all you who labor and are heavy laden, and I will give you rest."

If you truly believe in Jesus, He will always be with you. What a comforting feeling to know that despite whatever problems we are faced with, our Lord is with us as long as we place our faith and trust in Him. After all, He came to us because of His extreme love for all of mankind.

Forgiveness

God forgives us our wrongdoings and expects us to show love and forgiveness toward others. At times, we all find it difficult to forgive. The deeper the hurt, the more difficult it is to forgive. For example:

Maybe someone doesn't want you in their life anymore.

Maybe you told a friend something in confidence, and that confidence was violated.

Maybe you are a victim of malicious rumors resulting in character assassination.

> *The first to apologize is the bravest.*
>
> *The first to forgive is the strongest.*
>
> *The first to forget is the happiest.*[2]

> Judge not, and you shall not be judged. Condemn not, and you shall not be condemned. Forgive, and you will be forgiven.
>
> – Luke 6:37

Can you forgive? If you find it difficult to do so, think of Jesus dying on the cross. He asked God the Father to forgive those who crucified Him: "Father, forgive them, for they do not know what they do" (**Luke 23:34**).

Forgiveness for many does not come easily. There are numerous reasons for that, but one of the foremost is the difficulty in letting go of the anger, hatred, and any desire for revenge. If you are having trouble forgiving, seek God, ask for His help, continue to ask, and be patient. It will happen, and when it does, you will feel the relief of a spiritual illness that has been cured. If God can forgive us for the hurt we give Him every time we sin, then we should be able to forgive others. Not only should we, but we *must*, or we cannot expect forgiveness from God.

The gospel message is quite clear. In the Lord's prayer given to us by Jesus, He says, "Forgive us our sins, as we have forgiven those who sin against us" (**Matthew 6:12 NLT**). Jesus goes on to say, "For if you forgive men their trespasses, your heavenly Father will also forgive you. But if you do not forgive men their trespasses, neither will your Father forgive your trespasses" (**Matthew 6:14–15**).

Many examples of love and forgiveness can be found throughout the New Testament. In **Luke**

15:11–32, in the parable of the lost son, the love and forgiveness a father had for his son is clearly shown. Every time we sin, we are the lost son. When we realize that we were wrong and want forgiveness, our Lord is there for us. He welcomes us back home.

For our spiritual and physical well-being, forgiveness is a must. By forgiving we are taking a major step toward our goal—eternal salvation. By not forgiving we are limiting or eliminating achieving that goal.

It is through God's unconditional love for us that our past sins, when confessed, are forgotten. Ask His forgiveness and put a sincere effort into changing sinful ways.

> But if a wicked man turns from all his sins which he has committed, keeps all My statutes, and does what is lawful and right, he shall surely live; he shall not die. None of the transgressions which he has committed shall be remembered against him; because of the righteousness which he has done, he shall live.
>
> **– Ezekiel 18:21–22**

The way we conduct ourselves in the future will be a true expression of our love for God and our thankfulness for His forgiveness.

Daily Life

We can change our ways by bringing God into our everyday life. Through His help, bad habits can be broken, and good ones formed. One way of accomplishing that is through daily prayer. Ask God for the strength and courage to move forward. He is there waiting to hear from us. All we have to do is ask for His guidance.

The apostle Paul is an example of a complete change in one's life. Paul of Tarsus was one of the greatest Christian disciples of all times. He was a Jew and a Roman citizen. Prior to his conversion, he was known as Saul.

Paul was a formative enemy of the early followers of Jesus. It was during his journey to Damascus when his mission in life had a complete reversal. He was going there for one purpose and that was to eliminate the existing Christian community. However, it was not to be, for while on his way, Jesus appeared to him, and his life was changed forever.

Now it happened, as I journeyed and came near Damascus at about noon, suddenly a great light from heaven shone around me. And I fell to the ground and heard a voice saying to me, "Saul, Saul, why are you persecuting Me?" So I answered, "Who are You, Lord?" And He said to me, "I am Jesus of Nazareth, whom you are persecuting." And those

who were with me indeed saw the light and were afraid, but they did not hear the voice of Him who spoke to me. So I said, "What shall I do, Lord?" And the Lord said to me, "Arise and go into Damascus, and there you will be told all things which are appointed for you to do."

– Acts 22:6–10

He was no longer filled with hatred toward the believers of Jesus but was filled with love, forgiveness, and compassion. His faith was unshakable, and his determination to spread the teachings of Jesus consumed all the remaining years of his life.

Faith—A Necessary Part

It was while Paul was in Rome, in prison awaiting execution, that he summed up his life in a letter written to Timothy: "I have competed well; I have finished the race; I have kept the faith. From now on the crown of righteousness awaits me" (**2 Timothy 4:7–8 NET**).

"I competed well"

Paul was competing with the non-believers who by far exceeded the followers of Christ. During the first century, the world was primarily a pagan society. He was competing against those who persecuted, imprisoned, and finally executed him.

"I have finished the race"

Paul completed his race by his devotion to our Lord, his preaching of the gospel that resulted in the conversion of thousands of non-believers, and his establishing Christian communities from Jerusalem to Rome. It took him many years of hardship, but he never doubted his mission in life and always kept his faith and love for Jesus Christ.

We, too, are frequently competing against those who do not accept the teachings of Jesus. We are also competing against temptation, which at times can be like a "tug of war" between good and evil. Because of our human nature, that battle will continue throughout our life, and every time we overcome the temptation, we are on our way toward completing our race. There are many ways to accomplish that goal, but they all must have the same essential ingredients—love and forgiveness. For, without love and forgiveness in our everyday life, it will be next to impossible to even enter the race, and if we don't enter the race, we have no chance of completing it.

When our time is getting near and our trip through life is winding down, will we be able to say, like Paul, "I have competed well. I have finished the race. I have kept the faith. From now on the crown of righteousness awaits me"?

If we try to lead a true Christian life through our actions and the compassion we show toward others, we will have finished the race and can then look forward to receiving our reward, which is everlasting life in paradise.

Maybe some will say, "I have plenty of time." But remember, you can't finish the race unless you start. Starting begins with a foundation of faith and trust in our Lord and then grows and expands throughout our entire life.

What is faith? Faith is an instrument God uses to bring salvation to His people because He loves us.

> Now faith is confidence in what we hope for and assurance about what we do not see.
>
> **– Hebrews 11:1 NIV**

> Although I was formerly a blasphemer, a persecutor, and an insolent man; but I obtained mercy because I did it ignorantly in unbelief. And the grace of our Lord was exceedingly abundant, with faith and love which are in Christ Jesus.
>
> **– 1 Timothy 1:13-14**

> Fear not, for I am with you;
> Be not dismayed, for I am your God.
> I will strengthen you, Yes, I will help you,

I will uphold you with My righteous right hand.

– Isaiah 41:10

The righteous cry out, and the Lord hears, and delivers them out of all their troubles. The Lord is near to those who have a broken heart, and saves such as have a contrite spirit.

– Psalm 34:17-18

Ask God for faith. He gives it freely.

So I say to you, ask, and it will be given to you; seek, and you will find; knock, and it will be opened to you. For everyone who asks receives, and he who seeks finds, and to him who knocks it will be opened.

– Luke 11:9-10

But without faith it is impossible to please Him, for he who comes to God must believe that He is, and that He is a rewarder of those who diligently seek Him.

– Hebrews 11:6

We never know when we will be called to meet our Maker. When that time comes and our final judgment takes place, will we have earned eternal salvation? It is up to us. If we let Jesus come first in our lives, not only will we have eternal salvation, but we also will have a more peaceful and happier life on earth.

Jesus told us many times during His ministry to be prepared. For example, in **Matthew 24:42**, He said, "Watch therefore, for you do not know what hour your Lord is coming."

Jesus is not telling us to lead a life of fear. He wants us to be happy and enjoy all that has been created for us. He is telling us to be aware that our earthly life will someday be over. Our next life will be forever.

Paul tells us in **2 Corinthians 4:18**, "For the things which are seen are temporary, but the things which are not seen are eternal." And James, in his letter, says, "Whereas you do not know what will happen tomorrow. For what is your life? It is even a vapor that appears for a little time and then vanishes away" (**James 4:14**).

Therefore, it is in our best interest to pay attention to the teachings of Jesus and to get on the fast track to salvation. This is the kind of race that you win by just finishing, and you finish by believing and living a Christian life.

We are in the process of finishing the race every time we can say with truth and conviction:

I believe that Jesus is the Messiah.

I believe that Jesus is the Son of God.

I believe that Jesus loves me.

I believe that Jesus suffered and died for me.

I believe that Jesus is my Savior and my hope.

I believe that if I follow Jesus's teachings, I will be saved.

Jesus told us, "Peace I leave with you, My peace I give to you; not as the world gives do I give to you. Let not your heart be troubled, neither let it be afraid" (**John 14:27**).

The Beatitudes

The road to salvation is achievable for all people if we lead our lives according to the laws of God the

Father and the teachings of Jesus. His teachings are divine and have been revealed to us through God. They are the pathway to our crown of glory. We cannot pick and choose which ones to live by. If we say we are Christians and truly believe, then we must acknowledge and live by all His teachings. They are known as the *Beatitudes*, meaning "blessings," and can be found in **Matthew 5:1–12**:

> Blessed are the poor in spirit, for theirs is the kingdom of heaven.

("Poor in spirit" means we understand our need for God, who He is, and who we are.)

> Blessed are those who mourn, for they shall be comforted.

("Mourn" means sad because of sin.)

> Blessed are the meek, for they shall inherit the earth.

("Meek" refers to those who are patient and trust in the Lord.)

> Blessed are those who hunger and thirst for righteousness, for they shall be filled.

(This refers to those who want to do the right thing.)

> Blessed are the merciful, for they shall obtain mercy.

(This refers to those who are kind, forgiving, and compassionate.)

> Blessed are the pure in heart, for they shall see God.

("Pure in heart" are those who are truly righteous and not pretending.)

> Blessed are the peacemakers, for they shall be called sons of God.

> Blessed are those who are persecuted for righteousness' sake, for theirs is the kingdom of heaven.

The apostle James states that "for whoever shall keep the whole law, and yet stumble in one point, he is guilty of all" (**James 2:10**). And Jesus warned us that "not everyone who says to Me, 'Lord, Lord,' shall enter the kingdom of heaven, but he who does the will of My Father in heaven" (**Matthew 7:21**).

Christians Desire to Do Good

We accomplish the will of God by believing in Him. How we act is the true judge of our Christian character. Words alone can never replace good deeds, for they will be forever remembered by God. They don't have to be monumental in nature. They can be simple ones such as visiting a sick person, comforting someone in need, being kind, and forgiving others. After all, that's what a Christian life is all about. It is being humble, loving, and forgiving.

We can also, as Paul, be disciples of our Lord. Not only can we be disciples, but it is our responsibility to be so. Look what He is offering us: eternal salvation. That is our reward, but to receive it, we must earn it. He is not expecting us to go off to remote places and preach the gospel. Very few are chosen for that special mission in life. However, we can be disciples in thoughts, words, and actions. For example:

When we read and meditate on the teachings of Jesus, we are being His disciples.

When we take the time to talk about Jesus, we are being His disciples.

When we express our sincere love and forgiveness towards others, we are being His disciples.

> Therefore whoever confesses Me before men, him I will also confess before My Father who is in heaven.
> — **Matthew 10:32**

Being Jesus's disciple must begin with a strong foundation based on faith and trust in the Lord. It doesn't happen overnight, but through prayer and devotion to the Scriptures, it will grow on a continuous basis. Once that takes place, your life will be changed forever.

Hear what Jesus said about those who listen to Him and those who do not:

> Therefore whoever hears these sayings of Mine, and does them, I will liken him to a wise man who built his house on the rock: and the rain descended, the floods came, and the winds blew and beat on that house; and it did not fall, for it was founded on the rock.
>
> But everyone who hears these sayings of Mine, and does not do them, will be like a foolish man who built his house on the sand: and the rain descended, the floods came, and the winds blew and beat on that house; and it fell. And great was its fall.
>
> – Matthew 7:24-27

By truly believing in Jesus, we will establish a solid foundation of faith and trust in Him. He is our Shepherd, and we are His flock. Without Him to show us the way, we will be like the man who built his house on sand. It could not survive a severe storm and was washed away. That storm is sin, which, because of our human nature, will always be with us. We can, however, diminish its hold, and in many situations, because of our closeness to our Lord, eliminate it completely.

We face and will continue to be confronted with many storms of temptation during our lifetime, but with a solid Christian foundation they can be overcome. It will take time, but it's achievable. Our goal is to prevent wrongdoings from taking control of our lives and leading us into darkness and despair. The closer we are to God, the easier the fight against evil will be. Ask the Holy Spirit to give you the spiritual strength to win your battle against evil.

Moving Mountains

Jesus told us in Matthew 17:20, "If you have faith as a mustard seed, you will say to this mountain, 'Move from here to there,' and it will move; and nothing will be impossible for you."

We all have "mountains" to move out of our lives. Those are the thoughts, words, and deeds that are contrary to the teachings of Jesus. Jesus is telling us faith is so powerful that even with a small amount our demons can be defeated. Use the spiritual power of the Holy Scriptures to gain that faith.

The apostle Peter said, "The word of the Lord endures forever" (**1 Peter 1:25**). That "word" is found in the Holy Bible. It is the spiritual revelation of the past, present, and the future.

Prayer as a Vital Part of a Christian Life

Prior to reading the Bible, say a short prayer. Pray from the heart. Ask the Holy Spirit to give you the wisdom to understand the divine message. It is amazing what can be accomplished through prayer.

We all should try to make prayers a daily part of our life. They can be simple ones, just a few words like:

"Thank you, Lord, for all you have given me."

"Help me, Lord, to get through the difficulties of this day."

Just talk to God. Tell Him about your problems and ask for His help. He is always available and is waiting to hear from us and to help us through our problems regardless of how difficult they might seem.

We all face times of great distress. When we do, it is so easy to forget what God can work in our lives—sometimes in the most surprising way.

Prayers can be simple and your own words, or they can be the written thoughts of others. It doesn't matter as long as they have meaning and come from the heart. It is through prayer that we can move forward knowing we are never alone. God is always there. All we have to do is ask for His help: "Ask and it will be given to you; seek and you will find; knock and the door will be opened to you" (Matthew 7:7). What a comforting thought it is knowing that God is there for us.

Throughout our entire life, we will have many ups and downs. That is human nature. Our faith and devotion to God will help get us through the difficult times. We will never be given more than we can handle, and there will always be a way out. "We must through many tribulations enter the kingdom of God" (**Acts 14:22**).

In happy moments, PRAISE God.

In difficult moments, SEEK God.

In quiet moments, WORSHIP God.

In painful moments, TRUST God.

In every moment, THANK God.

– Rick Warren

Therefore whoever confesses Me before men, him I will also confess before My Father who is in heaven. But whoever denies Me before men, him I will also deny before My Father who is in heaven.

– Matthew 10:32–33

We acknowledge Jesus by truly believing and trusting in Him. Believing that He is the Son of God and because of His divine nature, is truly God.

The Lord's Prayer

One of Jesus's disciples asked Him, "Lord, teach us how to pray as John the Baptist taught his disciples." Jesus said to him, "This is how to pray," and He then taught them the Lord's Prayer:

> Our Father in heaven, Hallowed be Your name. Your kingdom come. Your will be done on earth as it is in heaven. Give us day by day our daily bread. And forgive us our sins, for we also forgive everyone who

is indebted to us. And do not lead us into temptation, but deliver us from the evil one.

– Luke 11:2-4

The Lord's Prayer is a simple prayer, but it's easy to recite it without thinking about the meaning of the actual words. Let's go through them.

"Our Father in heaven"

We are acknowledging that God exists and is in heaven. In fact, He **is heaven,** and as He is Jesus's Father, He is also our Father and Creator.

> "Let Us make man in Our image, according to Our likeness. ..." So God created man in His own image; in the image of God He created him; male and female He created them.

– Genesis 1:26–27

"Hallowed be Your name"

The name of *God* is holy and must always be held in the highest esteem, never should be taken in vain.

"Your will be done on earth as it is in heaven"

We should always try to do the will of God on earth, as the angels and saints do in heaven. We can accomplish that by following the Ten Commandments and the teachings of Jesus.

> I am the light of the world. He who follows Me shall not walk in darkness, but have the light of life.

> — John 8:12

"Give us this day our daily bread"

We are asking God to provide us daily with spiritual nourishment for our soul and physical nourishment for our body.

> And as they were eating, Jesus took bread, blessed and broke it, and gave it to the disciples and said, "Take, eat; this is My body." Then He took the cup, and gave thanks, and gave it to them, saying, "Drink from it, all of you. For this is My blood of the new covenant, which is shed for many for the remission of sins. But I say to you, I will not drink of this fruit of the vine from now on until that day when I drink it new with you in My Father's kingdom."

> — Matthew 26:26-30

"Forgive us our sins, for we also forgive everyone who is indebted to us."

God is all loving and forgiving. We will be forgiven in the same way that we forgive those who have offended us.

> For if you forgive men their trespasses, your heavenly Father will also forgive you.

But if you do not forgive men their trespasses, neither will your Father forgive your trespasses.

— Matthew 6:14-15

"And do not lead us into temptation, but deliver us from the evil one."

We are asking God to help us overcome the temptations of life through our faith and prayer.

With the Holy Spirit's help, these words can change our entire life, for the gospel message, love, and forgiveness, is the basis of this prayer.

Judgment

Jesus's love and forgiveness for all was stated many times during His ministry. When we find it difficult to forgive, think of Jesus dying on the cross. He said, "Father, forgive them, for they do not know what they do" **(Luke 23:34)**.

Not only do some of us find it difficult to forgive, but at times we can be too quick in passing judgment on others. God's judgment is the only one that means anything, and that will take place on the last day.

In **Matthew 7:1-2**, Jesus said, "Judge not, that you be not judged. For with what judgment you judge, you will be judged; and with the measure you use, it will be measured back to you."

The Deadliness of the Tongue

We know how destructive weapons can be, especially if they are not used for the right reasons. However, there is one weapon far more powerful and destructive than any that man has ever made. It is the human tongue. It is the malicious words spoken initially by a few, that can spread hatred from a city to a state to a country and finally throughout the world. It is the human tongue that caused the manipulation of mankind many times throughout history, resulting in persecution and attempts, many successful, to annihilate entire ethnic groups.

The apostle James, half-brother of Jesus, tells us:

> The tongue is a small part of the body, but it makes great boasts. Consider what a great forest is set on fire by a small spark. The tongue also is a fire, a world of evil among the parts of the body. It corrupts the whole body, sets the whole course of one's life on fire, and is itself set on fire by hell. . . . No human being can tame the tongue. It is a restless evil, full of deadly poison.
>
> **James 3:5–8 NIV**

Whatever happened to the teachings of Jesus?

Love One Another

On Holy Thursday, at the Last Supper, Jesus said to His apostles, "A new commandment I give to you, that you love one another; as I have loved you, that you also love one another" (John 13:34). He also said numerous times, "You must love your neighbor as yourself." If we could only do that, think of what a better world this would be. The only way the world can truly be changed is through mutual love for one another. To have true love for our fellow man, there should first be respect—including respect for different ethnic lifestyles and faiths. It is very easy for us to become narrow in our way of thinking. Remember that God created *all* mankind and loves each and every one of us unconditionally.

Love, forgiveness, compassion, and humility are basics of Christianity. By focusing on the teachings of Jesus, we will develop a true understanding of their meanings and our life will be enriched with His blessings.

Creation of Man

God's greatest creation was man. Not only did He create us, but He created our soul after His own image and likeness, a true expression of His love. He gave us the gift of life. Without it, there would be no eternal salvation.

> Then God said, "Let Us make man in Our image, according to Our likeness; let them have dominion over the fish of the sea, over the birds of the air, and over the cattle, over all the earth and over every creeping thing that creeps on the earth." So God created man in His own image; in the image of God He created him; male and female He created them.
>
> **– Genesis 1:26–27**

51

For God formed man to be imperishable. The image of His own nature he made him. But by the envy of the devil, death entered the world and they who are in his possession experience it.

— Book of Wisdom 2:23–24

By faith we understand that the universe was formed at God's command, so that what is seen was not made out of what was visible. ... And without faith it is impossible to please God, because anyone who comes to him must believe that he exists and that he rewards those who earnestly seek him.

— Hebrews 11:3, 6 NIV

Free Will

God placed us above all His earthly creations. He gave us a soul that will live forever. He created us as rational beings. He also gave us free will. Because of our free will, we have been given the ability to make choices.

It is not God's fault when things don't go as we wish. Sometimes we make the wrong choices. It is amazing how quick we are to blame God for our mistakes—and yet, when things go our way, how seldom it is that we thank Him. Everything we do should be done with enthusiasm. By doing so we are honoring God. He gave us hope, which is a spiritual pillar of faith.

It is so easy to look at things in a negative way. When that happens it usually sets the stage for a continuous flow of negative feelings, which in turn have a direct influence on our daily life and Christian faith. If we start our day with a negative attitude, chances are that we will have a negative day.

God didn't create us to be punished. He created us to enjoy the gift of life. With that gift comes faith and trust in Him, a God who loves us and will guide us if we let Him. God is our heavenly Father, our Creator. Thus, our soul has God's spiritual DNA. It is part of our spiritual make-up. Put that gift to good use and move forward in a positive manner.

Don't start your day with what you cannot do but with what you can and will do. We are a creation of the Almighty, who can only do what is good. Therefore, all human beings are a magnificent creation born with the gift of free will. That gift should be used wisely when making choices. If you have doubts concerning the choice you are about to make, ask yourself, *Is this what Jesus would do?*

God Wants Us to Be Saved

God is all-forgiving, and His love is unconditional. He is always there waiting for us to ask for His help and forgiveness. However, just because you say, "I'm sorry," and want to be forgiven doesn't mean that you will be. To be forgiven you must be sincere, and that sincerity must come from the heart. Above all, your sorrow for offending God must be genuine.

> "But if a wicked man turns from all his sins which he has committed, keeps all My statutes, and does what is lawful and right, he shall surely live; he shall not die. None of the transgressions which he has committed shall be remembered against him; because of the righteousness which

he has done, he shall live. Do I have any pleasure at all that the wicked should die?" says the Lord God, "and not that he should turn from his ways and live?"

– Ezekiel 18:21-23

That is a true expression of God's love and forgiveness. He didn't create us to be punished. We punish ourselves. It is not His intent to deprive us of salvation. He wants us to be saved, but how we lead our lives is our choice. God knows that we have at various times fallen out of His grace. However, because of His unconditional love, He is always there waiting for us to repent and receive His forgiveness.

If we are truly sorry, our confessed sins of the past are forgiven. No longer should we be burdened with a feeling of guilt. It will now be a new beginning with eternal salvation at hand. To help us achieve salvation, we were given the Ten Commandments. They are the laws of God given to Moses on Mt. Sinai and can be considered the tablets of life. Obey them and live forever in paradise.

Not only did God give us the Ten Commandments but, because of His unconditional love for us, He sent His only Son, Jesus Christ, to suffer and die for our sins so that we could be saved.

For God so loved the world that he gave his one and only Son, that whoever believes in him shall not perish but have eternal life. For God did not send his Son into the world to condemn the world, but to save the world through him. Whoever believes in him is not condemned, but whoever does not believe stands condemned already because they have not believed in the name of God's one and only Son.

– John 3:16–18 NIV

For the law was given through Moses; grace and truth came through Jesus Christ.

– John 1:17

Jesus Is God

Jesus is the most amazing person ever to walk the face of the earth. His miracles and teachings show His divine authority and wisdom.

He performed them out of love and compassion for mankind. By doing so, He clearly showed that He is the Messiah, the only Son of God.

But Jesus also demonstrated He is the same as God. Jesus told the Jews who were trying to arrest Him for blasphemy, "If I do not do the works of My Father, do not believe Me; but if I do, though you do not believe Me, believe the works, that you may know and believe that the Father is in Me, and I in Him" (**John 10:37–38**). He went on to say, "I and My Father are one" (**John 10:30**).

Earlier He had told the Jews, "I say to you, before Abraham was, I AM" (**John 8:58**). When He said this, they picked up stones to throw at Him because His use of "I AM" was equating Himself with God, which the Jews considered blasphemy— deserving of death.

Jesus Performed Miracles

A few of the many miracles Jesus performed are:

– Turning water into wine – **John 2:1–12**

- Walking on water – **Matthew 14:25**

- Feeding the five thousand – **Matthew 14:13**

- Healing of a leper – **Luke 5:12–14**

- Healing a blind man – **Mark 8:22–26**

- Raising Lazarus from the dead – **John 11:38–44**

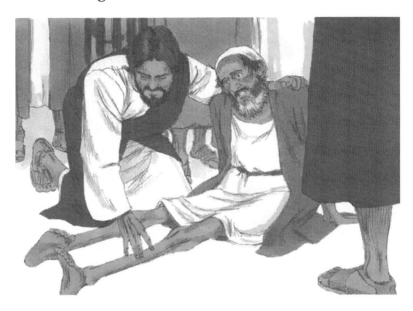

Jesus's ministry lasted only three years, and during that time He preached love and forgiveness for all mankind. He set the example for us to live by. It is through the power of His outpouring grace that we can move forward with our lives, free from the guilt of the past and full of anticipation for the future. His grace is always available and will enter our hearts through the sincerity of our daily prayers.

It most likely will not happen overnight, but it will happen, and gradually our outlook on life will have forever changed.

> This is My commandment, that you love one another as I have loved you. Greater love has no one than this, than to lay down one's life for his friends. You are My friends if you do whatever I command you.
>
> — John 15:12–14

The Four Gospels

The Christian Gospels, the good news, written by Matthew, Mark, Luke and John, describe the birth, life, ministry, crucifixion, and resurrection of Jesus. They are the recorded history of Jesus's life on earth and His teachings.

Matthew was called by Jesus to be an apostle while sitting in the tax collector's office at Capernaum. As Jesus was passing by, He simply said, "Follow Me," which Matthew immediately did without question (**Matthew 9:9**). Matthew's Gospel was written in Hebrew sometime before AD 50 and was translated into Greek prior to AD 100.

Matthew wrote his Gospel for those who believed in Jesus and for those who did not. For the believers, it strengthens their spiritual lives, and for the non-believers it was a means of convincing them that Jesus was the Messiah. Matthew gave his life for Jesus by being martyred in Ethiopia.

Mark and his mother were both very active in the early development of Christianity. In fact, his mother's house in Jerusalem served as a meeting place for the followers of Christ. Mark was a missionary and secretary to Peter. While in Rome he wrote his Gospel. He wrote it for the Romans sometime before AD 60 to show them that Jesus is our Savior and that He is divine.

His Gospel is a record of the life of Jesus as seen through the eyes of Peter, one of the apostles (along with the brothers James and John) in Jesus's inner circle. Mark also was a personal witness to many of the miracles performed by Jesus. He suffered martyrdom in Egypt where he was dragged by horses through the streets until he was dead.

Luke was born in Antioch, Syria. He was a physician and among the earliest converts to Christianity. He was a missionary and together with Paul was responsible for the conversion of many non-believers and the establishment of numerous Christian communities. His Gospel was written prior to AD 60 and was intended to show the converts the solid foundation their faith had. His Gospel is based on the facts gathered from those who had been witness to the ministry of Jesus. Luke was hanged while in Greece because of his faith.

John was a fisherman who came from the town of Bethsaida. While passing by, Jesus called to John and his brother, James, and they immediately left their fishing boat and followed Him (**Matthew 4:20– 22**). Jesus was very close to John. In fact, prior to His death, He entrusted to him the care of His mother, the Blessed Virgin.

John faced martyrdom in Rome but survived. He was then sentenced to the mines on the island of Patmos. Later he was freed and became the first Bishop of Edessa in Turkey. He lived to an old age, and it was during his old age that he wrote his Gospel.

It should be noted that Matthew and John were chosen apostles of Jesus. What is written is what they experienced while being with Him during His entire ministry. They were firsthand witnesses to the many miracles and to the thousands who gathered to hear Jesus preach.

There are people who doubt the Gospels. Some of the doubters are Christians who have difficulty in accepting the resurrection of Jesus. If you are one of them, ask yourself why the New Testament writers and many other believers suffered torture and death if the resurrection was fiction? If Jesus did not rise from the dead as He said He would, why would His apostles and numerous others who witnessed His resurrection suffer and die for a lie? Why, as some believe, would the apostles bribe the Roman guards at the tomb and remove Jesus's body only to die themselves for a lie? It just doesn't make sense. Jesus most certainly was crucified, died, and on the third day rose from the dead as both body and spirit. By doing so He fulfilled the many prophies of the Old Testament and gave us eternal life.

Salvation—A Free Gift of God

Frequently during Jesus's ministry, He was asked how we can achieve salvation. In Luke's Gospel, He answers that question:

And behold, a certain lawyer stood up and tested Him, saying, "Teacher, what shall I do to inherit eternal life?"

He said to him, "What is written in the law? What is your reading of it?"

So he answered and said, "'You shall love the Lord your God with all your heart, with all your soul, with all your strength, and with all your mind,' and 'your neighbor as yourself.'"

And He said to him, "You have answered rightly; do this and you will live."

But he, wanting to justify himself, said to Jesus, "And who is my neighbor?"

Then Jesus answered and said: "A certain man went down from Jerusalem to Jericho, and fell among thieves, who stripped him of his clothing, wounded him, and departed, leaving him half dead. Now by chance a certain priest came down that road. And when he saw him, he passed by on the other side. Likewise a Levite, when he arrived at the place, came and looked, and passed by on the other side.

But a certain Samaritan, as he journeyed, came where he was. And when he saw him, he had compassion. So he went to him and bandaged his wounds, pouring on oil and wine; and he set him on his own animal, brought him to an inn, and took care of him. On the  next day, when he departed, he took out two denarii, gave them to the innkeeper, and said to him, 'Take care of him; and whatever more you spend, when I come again, I will repay you.' So which of these three do you think was neighbor to him who fell among the thieves?"

And he said, "He who showed mercy on him."

Then Jesus said to him, "Go and do likewise."

– Luke 10:25–37

We, too, are being good Samaritans by being considerate and caring of others' needs. It is easy to look the other way. If we do, we disregard what Jesus told us: "Love your neighbor as yourself." That love is shown by respecting all people and eliminating hatred from our everyday existence. By doing so, we will experience a peace and contentment in our lives.

Jesus promised us salvation and eternal life many times during His ministry:

> Most assuredly, I say to you, if anyone keeps My word he shall never see death.
>
> — John 8:51

Jesus is talking about eternal death, which is caused by serious sin.

> Even so must the Son of Man be lifted up, that whoever believes in Him should not perish but have eternal life.
>
> — John 3:14-15

> Then Jesus spoke to them again, saying, "I am the light of the world. He who follows Me shall not walk in darkness, but have the light of life."
>
> — John 8:12

It is because of Jesus's death, resurrection, and ascension into heaven that our salvation is possible.

Faith and Hope

Jesus gave us the foundation of faith to build on. He also gave us hope, a divine beacon forever shinning bright and always guiding us to Him.

> Blessed is the man who trusts in the Lord, and whose hope is the Lord.
>
> **– Jeremiah 17:7**

Faith is what Christianity is based on; it is a gift from God. Hope is a "spiritual pillar" of faith. It is belief and trust, and with that belief and trust comes loyalty, which is our allegiance to God.

> Now faith is the substance of things hoped for, the evidence of things not seen.
>
> **– Hebrews 11:1**

> So then faith comes by hearing, and hearing by the word of God.
>
> **– Romans 10:17**

Without faith, our spiritual being is in a constant state of turmoil. It is through faith that we hear the voice of the Lord. He is always with us if we believe in Him. To believe in Him, we must know Him, and to know Him is to hear Him. To hear Him is a spiritual feeling—not actual spoken words but an inner knowledge of His presence.

Have you ever thought of visiting a house of worship at a time of day when you will most likely be the only one there? Just enter, sit, and enjoy the peace and quiet. It is just you and God. You don't even have to pray. God knows you are there, and He will communicate in His own way. Maybe just a warm feeling or a sudden solution to a lingering problem. But none of this comes to be without a continuous sincere effort on our part.

- It is because of our faith we believe that God created the universe and everything in it.

- It is because of our faith we believe that God created us after His own image and likeness.

- It is because of our faith we believe that God created us with a soul that will live forever.

- It is because of our faith we believe that God sent His only Son, Jesus Christ, to suffer and die for us so that we can have eternal salvation.

For "whoever calls on the name of the Lord shall be saved."

– Romans 10:13

Faith During Difficult Times

I have listed below some Scripture verses that will help you through difficult times:

Now the Lord is the Spirit; and where the Spirit of the Lord is, there is liberty.

– 2 Corinthians 3:17

Now faith is the substance of things hoped for, the evidence of things not seen.

– Hebrews 11:1

Be strong and of good courage, do not fear nor be afraid of them; for the Lord

68

your God, He is the One who goes with you. He will not leave you nor forsake you.

– **Deuteronomy 31:6**

Fear not, for I am with you; Be not dismayed, for I am your God. I will strengthen you, Yes, I will help you, I will uphold you with My righteous right hand.

– **Isaiah 41:10**

The righteous cry out, and the Lord hears, and delivers them out of all their troubles. The Lord is near to those who have a broken heart, and saves such as have a contrite spirit.

Psalm 34:17-18

Trust in the Lord with all your heart, and lean not on your own understanding; In all your ways acknowledge Him, and He shall direct your paths.

– **Proverbs 3:5–6**

Therefore humble yourselves under the mighty hand of God, that He may exalt you in due time, casting all your care upon Him, for He cares for you. Be sober, be vigilant; because your adversary the devil walks about like a roaring lion, seeking whom he may devour. Resist him, steadfast in the faith, knowing that the same sufferings are experienced by your brotherhood in the world. But may the God of all grace, who called us to His eternal glory by Christ Jesus, after you have suffered a while, perfect, establish, strengthen, and settle you.

– 1 Peter 5:6–10

Have you not known?
Have you not heard?
The everlasting God, the Lord,
The Creator of the ends of the earth,
Neither faints nor is weary.
His understanding is unsearchable.
He gives power to the weak,
And to those who have no might He increases strength.
Even the youths shall faint and be weary,
And the young men shall utterly fall,
But those who wait on the Lord
Shall renew their strength;
They shall mount up with wings like eagles,
They shall run and not be weary,
They shall walk and not faint.

– Isaiah 40:28–31

It is through our knowledge of Jesus that hope can have a meaningful place in our lives. We can travel along the road of life with Jesus at our side guiding us, or we can attempt to go it alone. It is our choice. If we take the latter approach, it usually results in an unbalance between our material and spiritual values. At some time, our travel through this life will end, and we will face our Maker. It is then that the life choices we have made will play a major part in determining our eternal fate.

Hope in God

Along with the gift of life, God gave us the ability to achieve worthwhile goals. He has given us hope.

Each of us, if we are able, has an obligation to use our God-given abilities. The major obstacle we must overcome is self-doubt. Self-doubt about ourselves and our abilities is something we all experience and will continue to do so as long as we are on this earth. Self-doubt is like a cancer—if not treated it will consume us.

And how is it treated? It is treated by trusting fully in God. That trust becomes a spiritual foundation that will give us the strength to understand our doubts and overcome their hold on us. To do that, we must push aside the negative and develop a positive attitude about our abilities.

For every negative thing we say, God has a positive answer.

When we say: *It's impossible.*

God says: *All things are possible.*

> "The things which are impossible with men are possible with God."
>
> — Luke 18:27

When we say: *I can't go on.*

God says: *My grace is sufficient.*

> "My grace is sufficient for you, for My strength is made perfect in weakness."
>
> — 2 Corinthians 12:9

When we say: *I can't figure things out.*

God says: *I will show you the way.*

> Trust in the Lord with all your heart, and lean not on your own understanding; In all your ways acknowledge Him, and He shall direct your paths.
>
> — Proverbs 3:5-6

When we say: *I can't do it.*

God says: *You can do all things.*

I can do all things through Christ who strengthens me.

– Philippians 4:13

When we say: *I'm always worried and frustrated.*

God says: *Cast all your cares on Me.*

Cast all your anxiety on him because he cares for you.

– 1 Peter 5:7 (NIV)

When we say: *I'm not smart enough.*

God says: *I give you wisdom.*

It is because of him that you are in Christ Jesus, who has become for us wisdom from God—that is, our righteousness, holiness and redemption.

1 Corinthians 1:30 (NIV)

When we say: *I feel all alone.*

God says: *I will never leave you as long as you believe in Me.*

Keep your lives free from the love of money and be content with what you have, because God has said, "Never will I leave you; never will I forsake you."

— Hebrews 13:5 (NIV)

When we say: *I can't forgive myself.*

God says: *I forgive you.*[3]

There is therefore now no condemnation to those who are in Christ Jesus.

— Romans 8:1

God wants to guide us through the difficulties we encounter. All we must do is ask for His help, have faith, and trust Him. If we are sincere, He will never let us down. Whatever comes our way will not be more than we can handle.

No temptation has overtaken you except such as is common to man; but God is faithful, who will not allow you to be tempted beyond what you are able, but with the temptation will also make the way of escape, that you may be able to bear it.

— 1 Corinthians 10:13

Ask Him what it is you should do with your life. You might not get the answer right away, and it might not be the answer you thought you wanted, but it will be what God wants. Be persistent in asking for help. Don't give up. Keep asking, and eventually you will find out what His plans are for you.

The more you ask and pray, the stronger your faith becomes, and as your faith becomes stronger, so does your relationship with Jesus. When that happens, you will realize that your life has taken a new direction. Anger and bitterness decrease, whereas humility, forgiveness, and love increase. Your life then becomes a more peaceful one because you know you are on the road to salvation.

Throughout life there will be many important choices to make, choices that will either drive us away from God or bring us closer to Him. Seek His guidance through prayer, and then prior to making the choice, ask yourself, *Is this what Jesus would do?* It then will become a lot easier to do what is right.

The solution to our problems is through Jesus. We are never alone. He is with us during our happy times, and He is with us during our difficult times. He is always with us if we believe in Him.

Making Choices

> Do not be deceived, God is not mocked; for whatever a man sows, that he will also reap. For he who sows to his flesh will of the flesh reap corruption, but he who sows to the Spirit will of the Spirit reap everlasting life.
>
> **– Galatians 6:7–8**

> Enter by the narrow gate; for wide is the gate and broad is the way that leads to destruction, and there are many who go in by it. Because narrow is the gate and

difficult is the way which leads to life, and there are few who find it.

— Matthew 7:13–14

Keep your life free from love of money, and be content with what you have, for he has said, "I will never leave you nor forsake you."

— Hebrews 13:5

To know that we can have Jesus with us always is a peaceful and comforting feeling, which will provide us with the strength and determination we need to lead a rewarding Christian life.

We should not dwell on the sins of the past. They will be forgiven if we are truly sorry that we have offended God and sincerely try to refrain from committing the same sin again. We must take responsibility for our actions, bring Jesus into our life, establish new goals, and trust in the Lord. God wants us to move forward and use the abilities He has given us to lead a productive life.

For I know the thoughts that I think toward you, says the Lord, thoughts of peace and not of evil, to give you a future and a hope.

— Jeremiah 29:11

Then He will also say to those on the left hand, "Depart from Me, you cursed, into the everlasting fire prepared for the devil and his angels."

— **Matthew 25:41**

If we confess our sins, He is faithful and just to forgive us our sins and to cleanse us from all unrighteousness.

— **1 John 1:9**

But if a wicked person turns away from all the sins they have committed and keeps all my decrees and does what is just and right, that person will surely live; they will not die. None of the offenses they have committed will be remembered against them. Because of the righteous things they have done, they will live. Do I take any pleasure in the death of the wicked? declares the Sovereign Lord. Rather, am I not pleased when they turn from their ways and live?

— **Ezekiel 18:21-23 NIV**

Everyone who believes in him receives forgiveness of sins through his name.

— **Acts 10:43 NIV**

Ask God to help you establish Christian values and goals. Ask from the heart.

How do we know what God wants us to do? Pray. Ask Him. Feel His presence.

So I say to you, ask, and it will be given to you; seek, and you will find; knock, and it will be opened to you. For everyone who asks receives, and he who seeks finds, and to him who knocks it will be opened.

– **Luke 11:9–10**

Money Vs. God

What we must be sure of is that we don't make the mistake of just acquiring material values and neglecting our spiritual values. For it is our spiritual values which will give us a solid Christian foundation and thus put us on the road to achieving everlasting life.

It is easier for a camel to go through the eye of a needle than for a rich man to enter the kingdom of God.

– **Mark 10:25**

This passage does not only relate to money, nor is it saying that a financially successful person cannot be saved. Once again, it is about values.

For the love of money is a root of all kinds of evil, for which some have strayed from the faith in their greediness, and pierced themselves through with many sorrows.

– **1 Timothy 6:10**

God gave each one of us the ability to do something positive with our lives, and that is good. It must be good because it is a gift from God. The difficulty takes place when material values take control and result in our living a lifestyle contrary to Christian teachings.

> For what profit is it to a man if he gains the whole world, and loses his own soul? Or what will a man give in exchange for his soul?
>
> – Matthew 16:26

Material values are temporary and usually bring happiness only for a short period before the desire for more and more takes place. When that happens, our spiritual values start to decrease, and our material values increase. We then find ourselves drifting further and further away from our Lord. An imbalance of values develops, which could lead to disastrous consequences. When the time comes for us to leave this earth, material values will be left behind and will be meaningless. That is not saying we should not enjoy the gifts God has allowed us to obtain. What it does mean is that they should not take the front row in our lives. It is through our spiritual values and not our material values that eternal salvation will be achieved.

> Do not lay up for yourselves treasures on earth, where moth and rust destroy and where thieves break in and steal; but lay up for yourselves treasures in heaven, where neither moth nor rust destroys and where thieves do not break in and steal. For where your treasure is, there your heart will be also.
>
> – Matthew 6:19–21

Conclusion

In summary, God loves us unconditionally, and He knows that our human nature is far from perfect. Our life is full of choices, and sometimes the wrong choices will be made. Not only does He love us unconditionally, but He is a forgiving God. He gave us His Son, Jesus Christ, to show us the way to salvation. If we follow the teachings of Jesus and obey the Ten Commandments, our crown of glory, eternal salvation, will be there for us.

Prayer of Faith and Guidance

O Lord, we thank you for allowing us to hear your word and feel your presence. We know you love us, and we want you to know that we love you. We are truly sorry for our sins, and we pray from our hearts for your forgiveness. Please, Lord, through the power of the Holy Spirit, give us the strength, courage, and wisdom to avoid any sinful temptations we might encounter. We also pray that you will guide us throughout our entire life in making the right choices so that we may achieve the reward you promised all mankind—eternal salvation.

Prayer for Avoiding Sin

Hear, Lord, the prayer we offer from grieving hearts. Have pity on us as we acknowledge our sins. Lead us back to the ways of holiness. Protect us now and always from the wounds of sin. May we ever keep safe in all its fullness the gift your love once gave us and your mercy now restores.

Prayer of Petition

Heavenly Father, may all people know your unconditional love. I pray especially for those who have no one to love them: the outcast, the oppressed, and the forgotten. Be their joy, Lord. Be their strength.

Prayer of Hope

Jesus, magnificent fountain of hope, in times of happiness and despair, you are the motivation of my heart, my hope of greater things to come. Transmit to my soul daily reminders to always hope for greater things. For without hope, life is futile. Hope is a spiritual pillar of faith, containing many rewards of its own.

Prayer of St. Augustine

May He support you all day long, till the shadows lengthen and the evening comes and the busy world is hushed and the fever of life is over and our work is done. Then, may He grant you a safe lodging, eternal rest, and peace at last.

Trust in the Lord

> My Lord God, I have no idea where I am going. I do not see the road ahead of me. I cannot know for certain where it will end. Nor do I really know myself, and the fact that I think that I am following your will does not mean that I am actually doing so. But I believe that the desire to please you does in fact please you. And I hope I have that desire in all that I am doing. I hope that I never will do anything apart from that desire. And I know that if I do this you will lead me by the right road, though I may know nothing about it. Therefore, will I trust you always though I may seem to be lost and in the shadow of death. I will not fear, for you are ever with me, and you will never leave me to face my perils alone.

> Thomas Merton, *Thoughts in Solitude*[4]

About the Author

Richard DeGiacomo has been married for sixty-one years to his wife, Elaine, and has three children, six grandchildren, and four great-grandchildren.

He served as a United States Marine and is a veteran of the Korean War. Richard attended Boston College, where he graduated with a bachelor's degree in economics. He has had an extensive business career.

For the last twelve years, Richard has been serving as a prison minister.

If you'd like to contact Richard, email him at achristianlife3@gmail.com.

THANK YOU for purchasing this book!

I would appreciate hearing from you! Your feedback helps to get this book into the hands of those who need it most. Online reviews are the biggest ways independent authors—like myself—connect with new readers.

If you enjoyed this book, could you please share your experience? Leaving feedback is as easy as answering any of these questions:

- What did you enjoy about the book?

- What is your most valuable takeaway or insight?

- What have you done differently, or what will you do differently, because of what you read?

- To whom would you recommend this book?

If you have a minute to share your experience, good or bad, please consider leaving your review!

I look forward to hearing from you!

Endnotes

---

[1] Mark Cahill, *One Heartbeat Away* (Rockwall, TX: BDM Publishing, 2005), 70–79.

[2] Author unknown.

[3] Author unknown.

[4] Thomas Merton, *Thoughts in Solitude* (New York: Farrar, Straus, Giroux, 2000).

Made in the USA
Columbia, SC
12 September 2021